I0815536

★★★★★
MLB TEAMS

Cincinnati REDS

KENNY ABDO

Fly!
An Imprint of Abdo Zoom
abdobooks.com

abdobooks.com

Published by Abdo Zoom, a division of ABDO, P.O. Box 398166, Minneapolis, Minnesota 55439.

Printed in the United States of America, North Mankato, Minnesota.
102025
012026

Photo Credits: Alamy, AP Images, Bridgeman Images, Getty Images, Shutterstock
Production Contributors: Kenny Abdo, Jennie Forsberg, Grace Hansen
Design Contributors: Candice Keimig, Neil Klinepier

Library of Congress Control Number: 2025936769

Publisher's Cataloging-in-Publication Data

Names: Abdo, Kenny, author.
Title: Cincinnati Reds / by Kenny Abdo
Description: Minneapolis, Minnesota : Abdo Zoom, 2026 | Series: MLB teams | Includes online resources and index.
Identifiers: ISBN 9798384940159 (lib. bdg.) | ISBN 9798384940913 (ebook) | ISBN 9798384941293 (read-to-me ebook)
Subjects: LCSH: Cincinnati Reds (Baseball team)--Juvenile literature. | Baseball teams --Juvenile literature. | Professional sports--Juvenile literature. | Sports franchises--Juvenile literature. | Major League Baseball (Organization)--Juvenile literature.
Classification: DDC 796.357--dc23

Table of CONTENTS

REDS

Led by powerhouse Hall of Famers who made the team royalty in the sport, the Cincinnati Reds have lorded over the Queen City and Major League Baseball (MLB).

14
4
REDS

As baseball's first professional team, the Reds have won World Series titles and featured legends, such as Johnny Bench and Barry Larkin, who helped build a winning **legacy**.

44

BATTER UP!

The first version of the Cincinnati Red Stockings formed in 1866. The team began paying players in 1869, becoming the first fully professional team in baseball and attracting some of the best players in the world. That year, Cincinnati finished 57–0. Sadly, the team would **disband** in 1870.

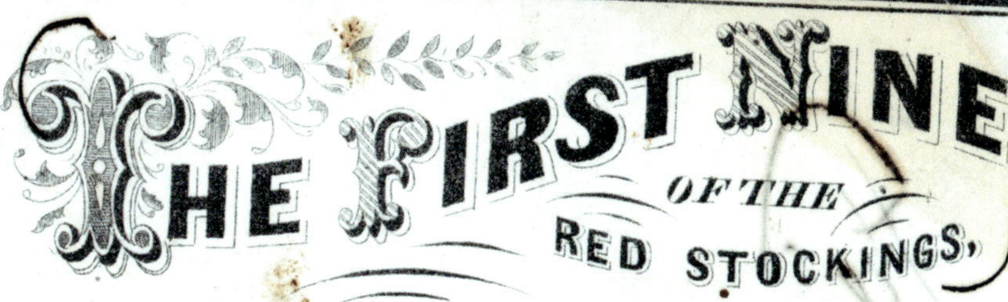

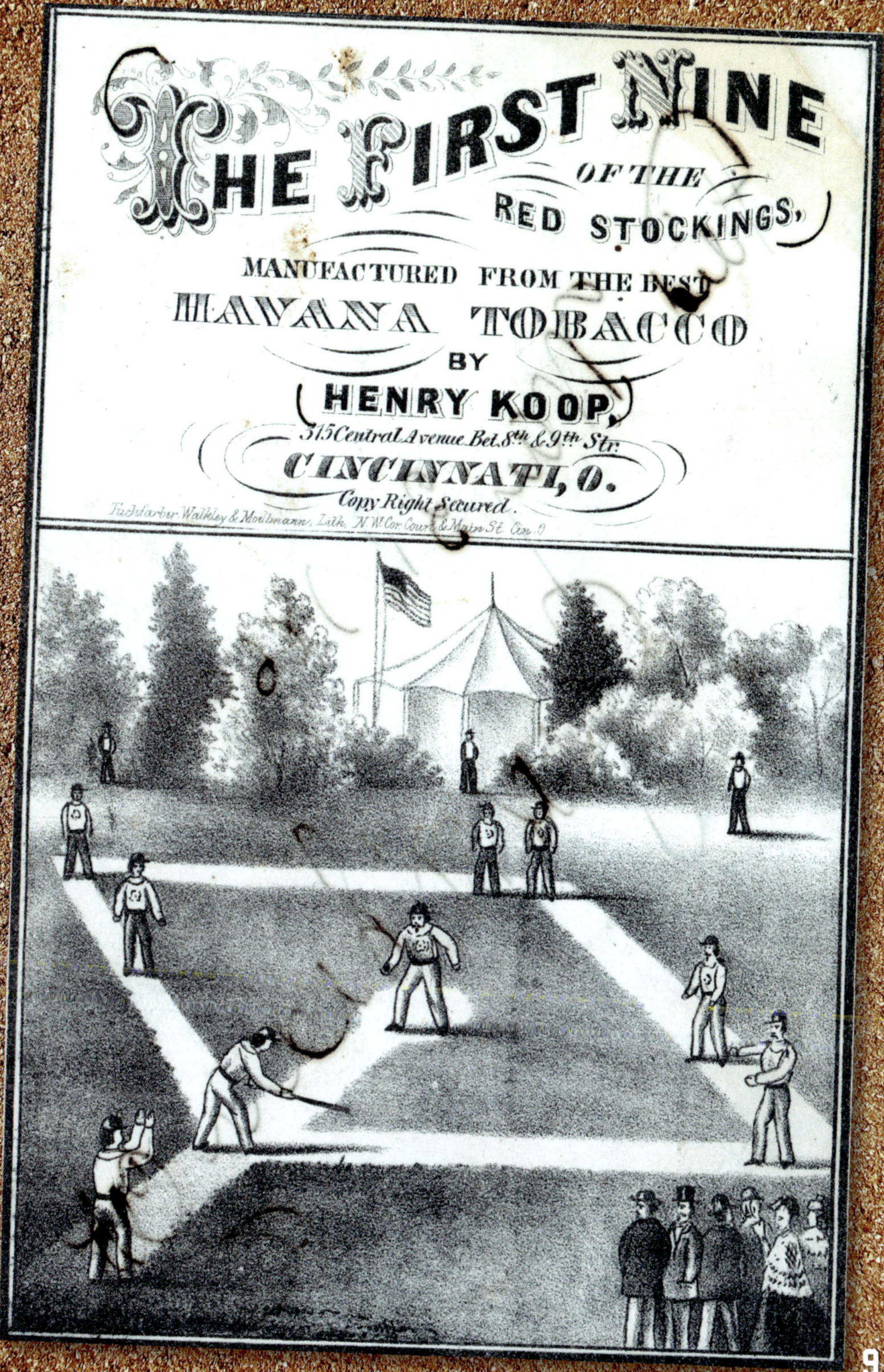
THE FIRST NINE
OF THE
RED STOCKINGS,
MANUFACTURED FROM THE BEST
HAVANA TOBACCO
BY
HENRY KOOP,
315 Central Avenue Bet. 8th & 9th Str.
CINCINNATI, O.
Copy Right Secured.
Tuchfarber, Walkley & Moellmann, Lith. N.W. Cor. Court & Main St. Cin. O

The next Cincinnati Red Stockings were original members of the **National League** (**NL**). The team was later kicked out of the NL for not following league rules. The team we know today was born in 1881. They later joined the NL for the 1890 season, shortening their nickname to the Reds.

In 1919, the Reds shocked the baseball world by winning the World Series against the White Sox!

But a dark cloud was cast over the victory. Known as the Black Sox Scandal, White Sox players were accused of losing on purpose.

GRAND SLAMS

The 1970s were an amazing time for the Reds. Nicknamed the Big Red Machine, the team was led by **manager** Sparky Anderson and stars like Joe Morgan and Pete Rose. The Reds dominated the field in those years, winning four **NL pennants**!

The 1975 team was one of the best baseball has ever seen. The Big Red Machine drove Cincinnati all the way to the World Series. The Reds won in a thrilling seven-game series against the Boston Red Sox!

The next year, the Reds **swept** the Yankees in the 1976 World Series. Johnny Bench won MVP and the team became the first to go undefeated in the **postseason**. The win cemented the Big Red Machine's **legacy** in Cincinnati and across baseball.

CINCINNATI
37

560 KSFO

After years of ups and downs, the Reds returned to glory in 1990. They **swept** the Athletics in the World Series and to prove they were back on top of the baseball world. José Rijo won MVP and the "Nasty Boys" bullpen helped shut down the A's.

Reds
21

The Reds won the **NL** Central title in 2010. Led by Joey Votto and Jay Bruce, the team won the **division** again in 2012. In 2020 and 2025, the Reds made it to the playoffs. However, both **postseasons** were short-lived due to offensive struggles. Cincinnati fans hope strong players like Hunter Greene are the key to a bright future.

HALL OF FAME

Johnny Bench spent his whole career with the Reds. He became known as one of the game's best catchers. He hit 389 home runs, won two MVP awards, and made 14 **All-Star** teams. Bench helped the Reds win two World Series and entered the Hall of Fame in 1989.

BENCH
5

Pete Rose, nicknamed "Charlie Hustle," got 3,358 of his **record** 4,256 hits with the Reds. Known for his nonstop hustle and clutch hitting, Rose made 13 **All-Star** teams and helped Cincinnati bring home three World Series titles.

CINCINNATI
14

RED

Joe Morgan was a superstar for the Reds, earning 10 **All-Star** selections and winning two World Series titles in 1975 and 1976. He also won two **NL** MVP awards and five **Gold Gloves**. In 1990, he was honored in both the Reds Hall of Fame and the Baseball Hall of Fame.

GLOSSARY

All-Star – a team consisting of athletes chosen as the best at their positions from all teams in a league or region or an athlete named to the contest.

disband – break up.

division – a number of teams grouped together in a sport for competitive purposes.

Gold Glove – an annual award given to the best fielders at each position in both the AL and NL.

legacy – the long-lasting impact of particular events that took place in the past.

manager – or field manager, the equivalent of a head coach who is responsible for overseeing and making final decisions.

National League (NL) – one of two 15-team leagues that make up MLB.

pennant – the title achieved by the team that wins its division or league championship.

postseason – the playoffs, including the wild-card round, divisional playoffs, league championship series, and World Series.

record – a top achievement by a team or player that no one has done before.

swept – to have won all games in a series.

ONLINE RESOURCES

To learn more about the Cincinnati Reds, please visit **abdobooklinks.com** or scan this QR code. These links are routinely monitored and updated to provide the most current information available.

INDEX